DATE DUE		
APR 2 4 '92		
JUL 9 '92		
SEP 1 0 '92		
OCT 1 '92		
JUL 6 '94		
NOV 9 '95		
MAR 1 9 '96		
APR 1 7 '96		
SEP 1 0 1998		
APR 4 2000		

ANIMAL FACT/
ANIMAL FABLE

Seymour Simon

ANIMAL FACT/ ANIMAL FABLE

illustrated by Diane de Groat

Crown Publishers, Inc. / New York

CROWN is a trademark of Crown Publishers, Inc.

Manufactured in Singapore

Library of Congress Cataloging-in-Publication Data
Simon, Seymour.   Animal fact, animal fable.
Summary: Describes common beliefs about animals and explains which are fact and which are
fable. 1. Animals—Miscellanea—Juvenile literature. [1. Animals—Miscellanea]
I. de Groat, Diane.   II. Title.   QL49.S517 1979   591   78-14866
ISBN 0-517-53794-X (paperback)
0-517-58846-3 (lib. bdg.)
10 9 8 7

For Joyce

INTRODUCTION

Many of us like to watch animals. You may have a pet dog or cat. At times you may notice that your pet moves its tail differently when it's happy than when it's angry. After watching your pet for a long time, you can probably tell a great deal about what each kind of tail movement means.

But even if you watch animals closely, it is sometimes easy to mistake what is happening. For example, a bat flutters around in an odd way in the night sky. Some people may think that bats are blind and can't see where they are going.

If bats are really blind, that belief is true; it is a fact. But suppose the bat flies in that odd way for another reason, and is not really blind. Then the belief is a fable; it is not true.

In this book, we'll look at some common beliefs about animals. Guess if each belief is a fact or a fable; then turn the page to find the answer. You will also discover why scientists think the belief is a fact or a fable.

FACT OR FABLE?

BATS ARE BLIND

FABLE In the night sky, bats seem to be blind. They fly back and forth in odd ways. But they are really catching tiny flying insects in the air. You can't see the insects in the darkness. You can see only the strange twisting movements of the bat.

Bats use their ears as well as their eyes to find their way at night. Most kinds of bats squeak in short bursts of high-pitched sounds. The sounds echo back from objects to the bats' ears and help the bats to catch insects on the wing.

SOME BEES STING ONLY ONCE

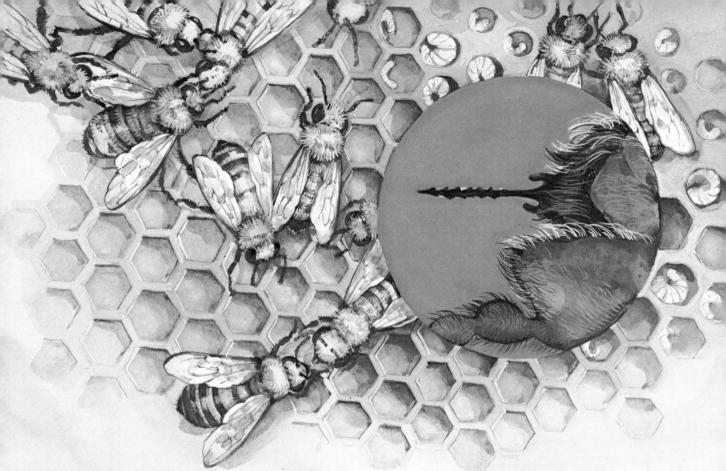

FACT Many kinds of bees can sting only once. A honeybee's stinger usually has barbs on it. The barbs are like tiny hooks. The barbs catch and hold fast. The stinger breaks off and remains behind. The bee dies after it loses its stinger.

A queen honeybee can sting again and again. Its stinger is long and thin and has no barbs. Male bees, called drones, have no stingers and cannot sting at all.

AN OWL IS A WISE BIRD

FABLE Some people think an owl looks wise because
of its wide-open eyes. But for a bird its size, the owl has
a tiny brain. If you say a person is as wise as an owl,
you are saying he is a birdbrain!

An owl moves its whole head when it looks around.
It never moves its eyes from side to side. Its eyes are
very sharp. It can see even small objects, such as mice,
that are very far away.

THE ARCHER FISH SHOOTS DOWN ITS FOOD

FACT The archer fish shoots down insects that live near the banks of streams and ponds. When an archer sees an insect, it swims toward it. The archer raises its mouth close to the surface of the water. Then it squirts a spray of water.

The water drops hit the insect and the insect falls into the water. One swift gulp and the insect becomes a meal for the finned sharpshooter.

A TURTLE CAN WALK OUT OF ITS SHELL

FABLE When people find an empty turtle shell on the ground, they may think a turtle left it behind and moved into a new one. But that is not true. A turtle can no more walk out of its shell than you can walk away from your ribs.

A turtle's shell is not just a house it lives in. The shell is really part of the turtle's body. You should not try to take a turtle out of its shell. If you do, the turtle will die. The empty shells you may find on the ground are the remains of turtles that have died.

A WOLF LIVES ALONE

FABLE The idea of the lone wolf is just a fable. Perhaps the story came about because single wolves were spotted from time to time raiding flocks and herds. But wolves really live together in close family groups and hunt in packs. Wolves keep the same mate for life. They are good parents. They take care of their cubs until the cubs are grown. Wolf packs even care for members of the pack that are too old or too sick to hunt.

SOME FISH CAN CLIMB TREES

FACT Most fish can't climb trees, but the mud skipper can. Skippers climb up logs or the branches of trees that lean into the water. Even when out of the water, skippers can breathe air through their gills.

The mud skipper lives in many parts of the world. It looks like a mixture of a fish, a tadpole, and a frog. Skippers use their thick front fins to skip about on the land. They are looking for insects and other things to eat.

CRICKETS TELL THE TEMPERATURE WITH THEIR CHIRPS

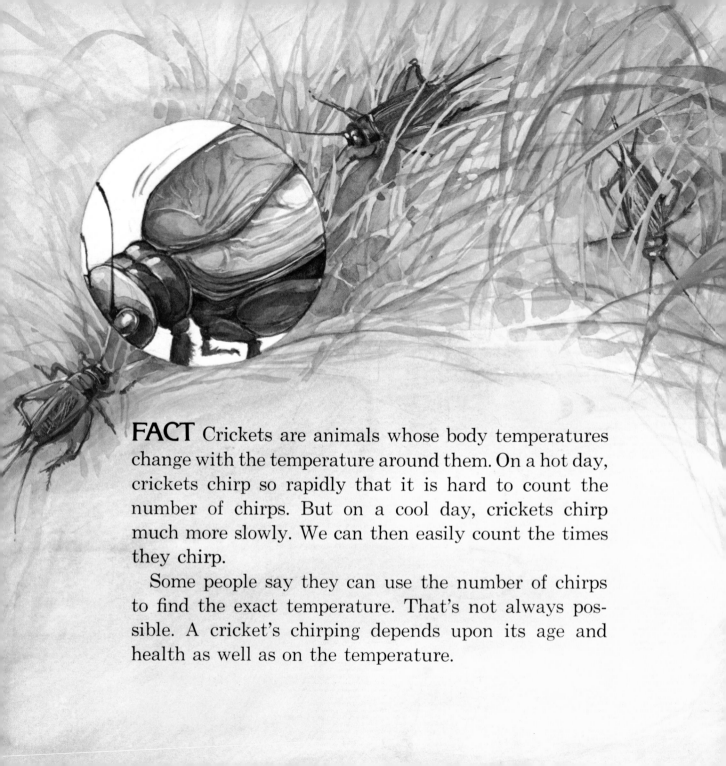

FACT Crickets are animals whose body temperatures change with the temperature around them. On a hot day, crickets chirp so rapidly that it is hard to count the number of chirps. But on a cool day, crickets chirp much more slowly. We can then easily count the times they chirp.

Some people say they can use the number of chirps to find the exact temperature. That's not always possible. A cricket's chirping depends upon its age and health as well as on the temperature.

ELEPHANTS ARE AFRAID OF MICE

FABLE We often see mice running about in elephant stalls in zoos and circuses. Sometimes the mice come very close to an elephant's trunk. Some people think elephants are afraid the mice will run up their trunks. But elephants seem to pay no attention to the mice.

Even if a mouse did run up an elephant's trunk, it would not hurt the elephant. The elephant would just blow out the mouse with one good sneeze.

A CAT HAS NINE LIVES

FABLE Since early times, people have said that cats have nine lives. In Egypt, a long time ago, cats were even thought to be gods. Cats are so quick and clever that sometimes it may seem as if the fable is fact. But cats, like all animals, have only one life to lose.

Many animals can hurt themselves if they fall from a height. But cats are so nimble that they usually land on their feet and walk away. Cats jump and move about so easily that it seems as if they are never hurt. Of course, that's not so. Cats do get hurt.

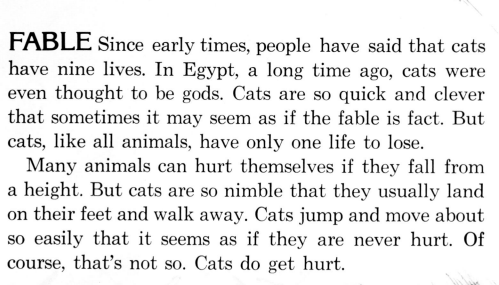

PORCUPINES SHOOT THEIR QUILLS

FABLE Porcupines cannot really shoot their quills. A porcupine's quills are sharp and have barbs like tiny hooks. The tip of a quill shown here has been magnified many times. When the quill sinks into an animal it becomes stuck and is left behind.

Porcupines use their quills to protect themselves. If an animal or person bothers a porcupine, the quills stand on end. The porcupine turns around and backs up to his enemy. Few animals bother a porcupine a second time.

DOGS TALK WITH THEIR TAILS

FACT We know dogs don't use words to talk, but their tails can tell us how they feel. When a dog wags its tail from side to side, the dog is happy and playful. But when a dog wags its tail up and down, it may be because it has done something wrong and expects to be punished.

If a dog keeps its tail straight up, be careful. That is the signal that it may attack. Don't run, just back away slowly.

OSTRICHES HIDE THEIR HEADS IN THE SAND

FABLE There is a well-known fable that ostriches stick their heads in the sand when they are frightened. Here's how the fable may have started. When ostriches see an enemy, they sometimes drop down and stretch out their necks along the ground. This makes it more difficult for the enemy to see them. To a person watching an ostrich, it may look as if the ostrich has buried its head in the ground.

An ostrich may not be very smart, but it is not dumb. When an enemy comes close, the ostrich gets up from the ground and runs away.

GOATS WILL EAT ALMOST ANYTHING

FACT Goats will eat almost anything they can find. They even seem to eat tin cans. But they are not really eating the metal can; they are chewing the label to get at the glue underneath.

Though goats eat string and paper, they would rather eat fruit, vegetables, grass, and leaves of plants. They are not quite the "garbage cans" some people think they are.

BULLS GET ANGRY WHEN THEY SEE RED

FABLE A bullfighter waves a red cape before a charging bull. Some people warn against doing something by saying, "It's like waving a red flag in front of a bull." You may have heard that a bull will attack a person wearing a red shirt.

There are many stories which tell us that bulls become angry when they see red. The trouble with these stories is that bulls are color-blind. It's the motion of an object in front of it that angers a bull. Bulls will get angry if you wave anything in front of them.

SNAKES CHARM THEIR PREY

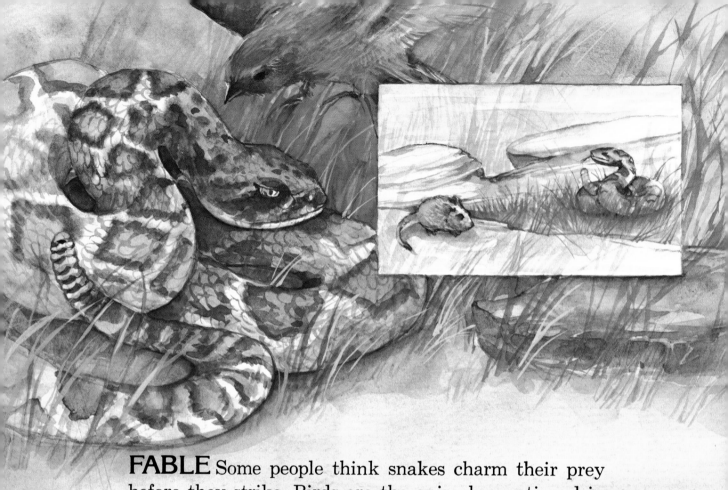

FABLE Some people think snakes charm their prey before they strike. Birds are the animals mentioned in most snake-charming stories. Sometimes a bird is seen fluttering around a snake's head. But it is not charmed. It probably is a mother bird seeking to draw the snake away from its nest and its young.

Small animals may "freeze" when they see a snake. But "freezing" for an instant is not the same as being charmed.

CAMELS STORE WATER IN THEIR HUMPS

FABLE A camel's hump does not hold water, it stores fat. The stored fat is used for energy when the camel doesn't get enough food.

But camels can go for days or even weeks without drinking water. Their woolly coats keep out the heat of the direct sunlight. The wool also keeps them from sweating and losing water too rapidly. A camel's body is just right for living in a hot and dry place.

SNAKES BITE WITH THEIR TONGUES

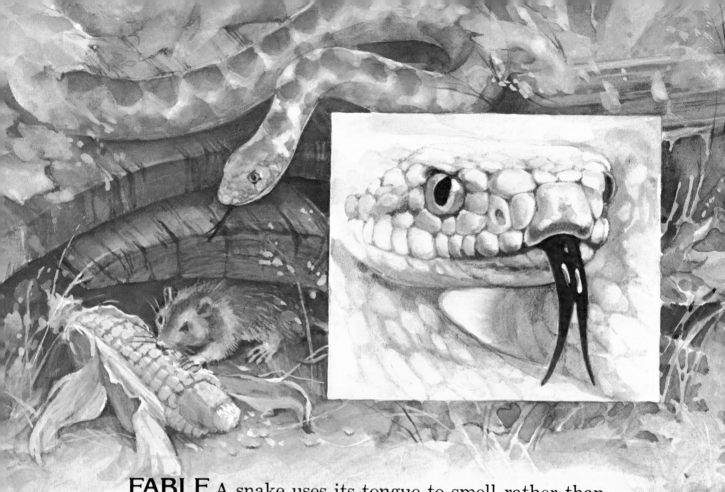

FABLE A snake uses its tongue to smell rather than to bite. Snakes have forked tongues that flick in and out. The forked tongue may look sharp, but the snake can't really bite anything with it. Its tongue is much too soft to cause an injury.

A snake's tongue picks up the smell of animals in the air. The tongue then carries the smell back into the snake's mouth. This helps the snake to track its prey.

RATS DESERT A SINKING SHIP

FACT It is a fact that rats will try to jump overboard if a ship is sinking. But that is true of any animal that can swim, and even some that can't. Rats sometimes desert a ship even if it isn't sinking. In the days of sailing ships, it was a common sight to see packs of rats jumping overboard.

Sailing ships were slow. They stayed at sea for many months. By the time a ship returned to port, there was little food left for the rats. When the ship came close to shore, the hungry rats would dive overboard and swim to land to find food.

RACCOONS WASH THEIR FOOD

FABLE Raccoons sometimes dip their food into water before they eat, but they are not washing it. A raccoon's throat is not very large. It has trouble swallowing large pieces of food. Dipping food in water makes it softer and easier to swallow. When a raccoon finds a mushy piece of fruit, he doesn't wash it no matter how dirty it is. He just gulps it down right away.